WORKING WITH
ANIMALS

by Susan M. Ewing

12 STORY LIBRARY

12-Story Library is an imprint of Bookstaves and Press Room Editions

Produced for 12-Story Library by Red Line Editorial

Photographs ©: Mike Price/Shutterstock Images, cover, 1; gkuchera/iStockphoto, 4; Zazaa Mongolia/ Shutterstock Images, 5; IvonneW/iStockphoto, 6; Fertnig/iStockphoto, 7; Nejron Photo/Shutterstock Images, 8; Tyler Olson/Shutterstock Images, 9; Lokibaho/iStockphoto, 10; John Roman Images/ Shutterstock Images, 11; marlenka/iStockphoto, 12; Marie Charouzova/Shutterstock Images, 13; ChameleonsEye/Shutterstock Images, 14; A_Mikhail/Shutterstock Images, 15; Melounix/Shutterstock Images, 16; Kari K/Shutterstock Images, 17, 29; enchanted_fairy/Shutterstock Images, 18; kali9/ iStockphoto, 19; hedgehog111/Shutterstock Images, 20; moosehenderson/Shutterstock Images, 21; subman/iStockphoto, 22, 28; Photology1971/Shutterstock, 23; turtix/Shutterstock Images, 24; Virginia State Parks CC2.0, 25, 27; a katz/Shutterstock Images, 26

Library of Congress Cataloging-in-Publication Data
Names: Ewing, Susan M., author.
Title: Working with animals / by Susan Ewing.
Description: Mankato, MN : 12 Story Library, [2017] | Series: Career files | Includes bibliographical references and index.
Identifiers: LCCN 2016047628 (print) | LCCN 2017006494 (ebook) | ISBN 9781632354525 (hardcover : alk. paper) | ISBN 9781632355195 (pbk. : alk. paper) | ISBN 9781621435716 (hosted e-book)
Subjects: LCSH: Animal specialists--Juvenile literature. | Veterinary medicine--Vocational guidance--Juvenile literature. | Zoologists--Vocational guidance--Juvenile literature. | Animal welfare--Vocational guidance--Juvenile literature. | CYAC: Vocational guidance.
Classification: LCC SF80 .E86 2017 (print) | LCC SF80 (ebook) | DDC 636.0023--dc23
LC record available at https://lccn.loc.gov/2016047628

Printed in the United States of America
022017

Access free, up-to-date content on this topic plus a full digital version of this book. Scan the QR code on page 31 or use your school's login at 12StoryLibrary.com.

Table of Contents

Animals Helped Prehistoric People

People have been working with animals for a long time. Researchers are not sure which animal humans succeeded in taming first. But the first animal humans may have worked with was the wolf. They were domesticated sometime between 30,000 and 16,000 BCE. These dogs may have helped early humans hunt.

In approximately 8000 BCE, humans began to farm. During this time, humans tamed several other animals. Some of them provided humans with a source of food, such as milk. Other animals helped humans farm. It was easier to plow fields using cattle and oxen.

Horses were one of the last animals to be domesticated. This happened in approximately 4500 BCE. People discovered they could ride horses. They could also use horses to pull wagons and plows.

Some farms use dogs to herd sheep.

43.3 million

Number of homes in the Unites States with a dog as a pet.

- People have worked with animals for thousands of years.
- Humans first worked with wolves and later with cows and horses.
- People who want to work with animals need to learn everything they can about them.

THINK ABOUT IT

Tamed wolves evolved into modern-day dogs. But some wolves remained wild. Are there other species of tamed animals that have wild relatives still living? Do a little research to find out more.

Today, people work with animals in a variety of ways. People who work with animals need to understand how to take care of them. They need to know what to feed them and how long an animal can work before it needs a rest. People who want to work with animals must learn all they can about them.

Wild horses at Hustai National Park in Mongolia

Pets Have Doctor Appointments, Too

Veterinarians are doctors for pets. Small animal veterinarians take care of dogs and cats. They also take care of other pets, such as rabbits, guinea pigs, and ferrets. Veterinarians set broken bones and perform surgery. Veterinarians order shots for animals to prevent disease. They also give medicine to help protect animals against parasites, such as fleas and ticks.

It takes a lot of work to become a veterinarian. Future veterinarians should focus on taking advanced math, chemistry, and biology classes while in high school. Then they need to attend college and earn a bachelor's degree. After college, students must apply to veterinary school. There are 30 veterinary schools approved by the American Veterinary Medical Association. Once accepted, students study for another four years.

After attending veterinary school, graduates must pass the North American Veterinary Licensing Examination. Some states have

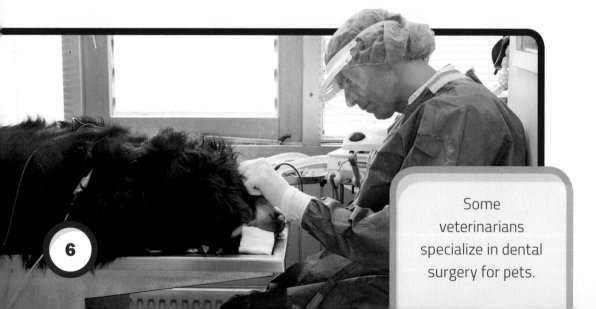

Some veterinarians specialize in dental surgery for pets.

It is often easier for large animal veterinarians to go to their patients rather than having the animals brought to them.

more requirements before veterinarians can earn their licenses. Those who want to specialize in a certain area, such as veterinarian dentistry, need to be certified. Once they are licensed, veterinarians can expect to earn between $50,000 and $109,000 per year.

40

Percentage of students accepted to US veterinary schools who applied in 2013.

- Small animal veterinarians are doctors for pets.
- Veterinarians have to complete many years of school.
- After finishing school, veterinarians have to pass an exam to get a license.

LARGE ANIMAL VETERINARIANS

Not all veterinarians treat pets. Some are specially trained to treat farm animals, such as cows, horses, sheep, and pigs. Large animal veterinarians help animals in many of the same ways small animal veterinarians do. They order vaccines and medicine, and they perform surgery. Large animal veterinarians do not usually work from an office, though. Instead, they travel from farm to farm to treat animals.

Vet Techs Keep Operations Running Smoothly

Veterinary technicians are nurses for animals. A veterinary technician is often the first person someone sees when taking a pet to a veterinarian. Veterinary technicians talk with animal owners. They record information about the health of pets. They usually weigh pets and may take their temperatures. A veterinary technician may be the one to cut a pet's nails.

Veterinary technicians do many jobs to assist the veterinarian. They help with operations. They may give anesthesia and monitor the pets. After a veterinarian prescribes vaccines and medicines, technicians

Veterinary technicians often weigh pets.

95,600
Number of US veterinary technicians in 2014.

- Veterinary technicians assist veterinarians and are like nurses for animals.
- Technicians need to have an associate's degree and may need to pass a state test.
- Compassion is an important skill to have when treating sick or injured animals.

year, so it is a good job for animal lovers. But technicians need to have other skills, too. Like nurses for people, veterinary technicians have to pay close attention to details. They also have to have compassion. Many of the animals technicians treat are sick and need help. Technicians need to know that most animals have a shorter lifespan than humans. They sometimes have to help owners say good-bye to their pets. But technicians often help pets feel better.

give them in the correct dose. They may draw blood and do laboratory tests. Some technicians take X-rays.

Veterinary technicians need to have an associate's, or two-year, degree in veterinary technology. Most states require technicians to pass a state test. After earning a degree, a person can decide what kind of animals to work with. Many technicians work with pets, but some work with farm animals or in a zoo.

Veterinary technicians earn an average of $30,000 a year. More technicians are needed every

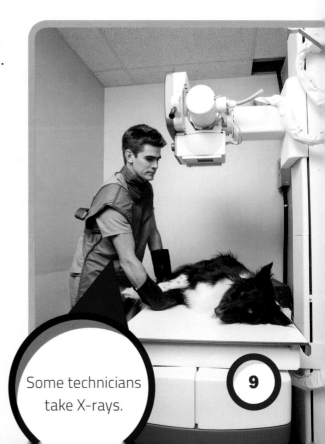

Some technicians take X-rays.

Dogs Can Be Humans' Eyes and Ears

Dog training is a perfect job for people who like dogs and helping others. There is no formal education or license for dog trainers. People can learn dog training at a special school, or they can learn from another trainer as an apprentice. There are many kinds of dog trainers.

Dog trainers must take care to not become too attached. The dogs they train are not pets. The animals are working dogs that will help people who are disabled or help police officers do their jobs. After training is complete, the dogs go home with their new handlers.

Some people train service dogs to help those with disabilities. Hearing dogs can alert their handlers who are deaf to common sounds,

Some service dogs can be trained to push crosswalk buttons for their handlers.

Police dogs usually retire by the age of 10.

such as a telephone call or the doorbell. Seizure response dogs can be trained to get help when their handlers need it. Because these dogs must remain calm, many service dogs are Labrador retrievers and golden retrievers.

Some dog trainers teach police dogs. Trainers have to teach the dogs how to guard suspects and detect drugs. After training, the dogs are matched with a police officer in a K9 unit. Police dogs must help their handlers in dangerous situations and keep them safe. For this reason, many police dogs are German Shepherds.

3

Maximum number of minutes a dog training session should last.

- Dog trainers do not need formal education.
- Some dog trainers work with service dogs that help people with disabilities.
- Other dog trainers teach police dogs.

Trainers Work with Young Horses

People who love horses sometimes become horse trainers. There are colleges that offer courses for horsemanship, but many trainers learn from experience. People who want to be trainers need to spend a lot of time riding horses. They need to ride all kinds of horses and learn as much as they can. Students can learn from people and from books.

People who are interested in horseracing begin working with a horse when it is just two years old. That means racehorses are still quite young when they begin their training. Young racehorses can become spooked or scared more easily than older horses. Good horse trainers know how to help racehorses feel less anxious. They also begin their training sessions early in the morning, while the air is still cool. This helps keep horses from becoming overheated.

Some horses are trained to compete in shows or to take tourists

Racehorses sometimes wear hoods to keep them focused on the race.

on trail rides. Trainers who work with these horses need to teach them more commands than racehorses have to learn. Show horses have to learn how to jump and work with a rope. People who work at ranches help horses learn to be comfortable with many different types of people. But all forms of horse training take a lot of work and patience.

Students can help at a stable in exchange for riding lessons. They might clean out stalls or clean saddles and bridles.

5

Minimum number of gallons (19 L) of water a horse should drink every day.

- Horse trainers can take college classes or learn from other trainers.
- Trainers start working with racehorses when the animals are very young.
- Show horses and ranch horses have to be taught more commands than a racehorse has to learn.

Horse camps can teach the basics of grooming.

Marine Mammal Trainers Spend Time in the Water

Working with animals that live in the sea may sound like fun, but it is not easy. Trainers need to work outdoors and be strong swimmers. Most trainers need to be certified scuba divers.

Some trainers work at theme parks, such as Sea Life Park in Hawaii. Other trainers may work at zoos, such as the Saint Louis Zoo. People who come to these places enjoy watching shows where sea lions dive off platforms and toss Frisbees. But the trainers do more than help marine animals perform in shows. The trainers clean pools, prepare meals for the animals, and keep records. They also give talks and

Handlers often use whistles when training dolphins.

Trainers help educate people about marine mammals.

teach people about the animals. Theme parks and zoos are open nights, weekends, and holidays, so trainers should expect to work during these times, too.

Most trainers need a college degree in some area of marine biology to be a marine mammal trainer. That is because trainers use the time during sessions to also check on an animal's health. An experienced trainer will make an average of $74,000.

60

Number of years Sparky the Sea Lion Show has been running at the Como Zoo in Saint Paul, Minnesota.

- Marine animal trainers need to be strong swimmers.
- Some work at theme parks, and some work at zoos.
- Trainers feed and care for marine animals in addition to training them.
- Most trainers need a degree in marine biology to find a job.

THINK ABOUT IT

To work with animals, some jobs require years of schooling. Others have on-the-job training. What are some of the benefits of learning from a textbook? What are some of the benefits of hands-on learning?

Trainers Speak to Animals Using Clicks

Animals do not speak. Humans do not talk in barks and hisses. So how do trainers tell animals what they want them to do? The answer is clicker training. Clicker training can be used to train any animal. It is a good way to train because it does not use force. It uses a sound to tell the animal it did the right thing. That sound is followed by a food reward. Many people use a small metal clicker to make the sound. People who train marine animals use a whistle.

To begin, trainers use the clicker and then immediately give the animal a treat. The trainers do this 8 or 10 times in a row. Now the animal knows the sound of the clicker means a treat will follow.

Many dog owners use clicker training when their pets are puppies.

TRAINING PIGEONS

Some might think that the first animal to be trained using a clicker was a dog. In fact, it was a pigeon. In 1943, scientists taught the bird to bowl using a tiny ball and tiny pins. To start, scientists used the clicker and rewarded the pigeon for just looking at the bowling ball.

Next, a trainer tries to catch the animal in the act of a certain behavior, such as sitting. The trainer then quickly names the behavior, uses the clicker, and then gives the animal a treat. Over time, the animal learns to do the same action when hearing the verbal command.

3

Maximum number of seconds between using the clicker and giving a treat.

- Clicker training can be used with any animal.
- The method uses a sound quickly followed by a food reward.
- Trainers using a clicker must be patient.

Trainers only train one animal for a few minutes at a time. They always end when the animal has done well. Trainers are always patient.

A trainer uses a clicker with a sea lion.

What to Do at the Zoo

There are as many types of jobs at zoos as there are animals. There are jobs working with large mammals, such as elephants and giraffes. Some people work just with exotic birds. Still others care for snakes, lizards, and turtles. Caring for these animals means knowing about their typical behavior, feeding them, and handling them when necessary.

How much education a person needs depends on the type of job. Most zookeepers need a bachelor's degree. Some zoos will overlook a lack of formal education if a person has years of experience taking care of animals. Being the head of an

A zookeeper feeds a red panda.

THINK ABOUT IT

Zoos give people a chance to see many different animals. Many of these animals would not survive if released back into the wild. These animals are safe in zoos, but they may not be happy. When is it okay to keep animals in captivity?

Zookeepers can help zoo visitors understand animal behavior.

entire department, such as birds, requires a degree in zoology or biology. That role also requires years of experience in a zoo. Veterinarians who work with zoos also have to be licensed.

A zoo job is a good choice for people who like working with wild animals. Those looking to get ahead should apply for volunteer positions and internships while in high school or college. Animals need constant care, so zookeepers should be prepared to work on weekends and holidays.

176,000
Number of jobs US zoos supported in 2016.

- There are many different jobs for animal lovers at the zoo.
- Most zookeepers need a college degree to find a job.
- Volunteer work and internships can help future zookeepers get ahead.

Doggy Daycare Is a Growing Business

Pet sitters take care of pets while the owners are away. Pet sitters may care for the pet at the pet's home, or they may take the pet to their own home. Dogs need walks, bathroom breaks, food, and fresh water. Cats need a clean litter box in addition to food and water. Fish may only need one visit a day.

In some places, pet sitters need a business license. It is a good idea for a sitter to have a contract. They should always put in writing what they will do for the pet.

Doggy daycare is a business that is becoming more and more popular. Many pet owners work long hours. They bring their pets to doggy daycare so their dogs can get exercise and socialize with other people and animals. People who want to work in doggy daycare need to know about different animal behaviors. They should learn how to help dogs who are anxious when away from their owners.

Formal education is not needed for pet sitting

Some pet sitters take care of unusual pets, such as hedgehogs.

PET SPAS

Some doggy daycares install cameras in their kennels and play areas. Owners can watch their pets even while at work. Others offer special snacks, grooming, and even doggy ice cream. Some doggy daycares have waterparks just for dogs.

or doggy daycare. But it is useful to know pet first aid. People who care for pets should write down all instructions from owners. They should pay special attention to any medications a pet may need.

$21,850
Average pay for an animal care worker in 2015.

- Pet sitters take care of pets while their owners are away, and some need a business license.
- People who work in doggy daycare make sure pets get exercise and attention while their owners are at work.
- Pet sitters and people who work in doggy daycare should know pet first aid.

This doggy daycare has a pool just for dogs.

Take a Walk with a Dog Buddy

Dog walking is a good way to work with dogs and also get exercise. There is more to it than just snapping a leash onto a collar, though. Dog walkers in big cities sometimes walk 10 or 12 dogs at a time. They need to know which dogs get along.

Dog walkers do not need formal education or a license, but they should still do some studying. Dog walkers need to learn all they can about animal behavior. They need to be able to tell if the dogs they are walking are happy or if they want to fight. Dog walkers also need to know the basics of obedience training.

Dog walkers help pets get the right amount of exercise.

They have to be able to control the dogs they are walking.

Dog walkers must help keep the dogs healthy. They offer dogs water after a walk. In the summer, they take walks in the morning when it is cooler. They closely watch dogs to make sure they do not overheat. In the winter, they help dogs stay warm. Where it snows, they help protect dogs' paws from salt and ice. And dog walkers should know pet first aid in case of an emergency.

$12
Average pay, per hour, for a dog walker.

- Dog walkers often walk more than one dog at a time.
- Dog walkers do not have to go to school or have a license.
- Knowing about dog behavior and obedience is important.
- Helping to keep dogs healthy is part of a dog walker's job.

Booties can help protect a dog's paws from salt and ice.

Naturalists Work Where the Wild Things Are

Nature preserves and centers can be owned and operated by cities, universities, and governments. One type of nature preserve is a state park. Biologists in parks work to count animals and to find where they live. This helps to protect animals. The biologists may band birds and bats. They may trap and mark turtles. They may ride in a helicopter to count deer.

Many cities have nature centers. These places often study the local ecology. They are natural areas for everyone to enjoy.

Naturalists have to be very knowledgeable about local wildlife. They often work closely with veterinarians. If someone brings in a wild animal that is hurt, naturalists bring the injured animal to a veterinarian who can help. Many nature centers are also home to animals that cannot be released back into the wild. For example, when a red-tailed hawk can no longer fly, it sometimes finds a home at a nature center. Naturalists are then

Every year, rangers at Custer State Park in South Dakota count the buffalo herd living there.

Raptor centers care for injured birds and release them back into the wild.

responsible for feeding and caring for these animals.

Besides knowing about wildlife, naturalists have to be able to write reports and speak in public. Most naturalists need a bachelor's degree to find a job.

Many nature preserves rely on volunteers and hire interns. This is a good way to learn about wildlife and about the jobs at nature centers. Most also offer classes and camps for kids and teens.

1916
Year the National Park Service was created.

- Nature preserves work to save wild spaces and the animals that live there.
- Naturalists have to be knowledgeable about local animals and plants.
- Working as a volunteer or intern is a good way to gain experience.

GET USED TO POOP

Working with animals means picking up poop. Barns, kennels, and cages need to be kept clean. Even jobs in the wild will involve poop. Poop can offer clues about what animal has been in the area. Wildlife biologists sometimes examine poop to see what an animal has eaten. It may seem funny, but poop can be important.

Get Started Now by Volunteering

Those who love animals do not have to wait until after high school to start working with them. Many state fairs have dog shows. At these events, handlers show off how well they have trained their dogs. Some dogs are judged on obedience, and some are judged on agility. Many of these dog shows depend on volunteers to keep the events running smoothly. Some state fair dog shows allow teenagers to volunteer.

Some animal shelters have many animals waiting for adoption. Very young dogs and cats need to spend time around humans to become good pets. Families can volunteer to foster shelter animals until they are adopted. Fostering is one way to gain experience caring for pets.

Many local nature centers offer programs for junior naturalists. Those interested in learning about the wildlife in their area can take classes. Junior naturalists can expect to learn how to identify common wild animals. Older teens can sometimes volunteer to care for animals that live at nature centers, such as injured birds.

Fostering an animal makes room for more pets at animal shelters.

7.6 million

Estimated number of animals living at shelters.

- People who volunteer at a dog show can watch dogs that are trained for obedience and agility.
- Fostering an animal is a great way to learn about the responsibilities of having a pet.
- Junior naturalists can learn about local wildlife by taking programs at nature centers.

4-H CLUBS

4-H clubs can offer young people hands-on experience with many different animals. 4-H is a national organization. There are local clubs in many parts of the country. Members can learn how to care for farm animals, such as cows, sheep, and goats. They can also learn about dogs, cats, and rabbits. And horse lovers can study horses.

These junior naturalists are learning about wetland animals.

Other Jobs to Consider

Animal Shelter Worker

Description: Walking, feeding, cleaning cages, washing dirty bedding
Training/Education: No formal education needed
Outlook: Growing
Average salary: $22,610

Pet Groomer

Description: Bathes and combs pets, as well as trims their nails
Training/Education: No formal education needed
Outlook: Steady
Average salary: $28,000

Show Dog Handler

Description: Conditions, trains, and grooms show dogs

Training/Education: No formal education needed; most trainers learn by working for a professional

Outlook: Steady

Average salary: $33,600

Zoologist / Wildlife Biologist

Description: Study wild animals and how they live, what they eat, and how they interact with nature

Training/Education: Bachelor's degree

Outlook: Steady

Average salary: $59,680

Glossary

agility
The ability to move quickly and easily.

anesthesia
A drug or gas used to prevent pain.

apprentice
A person who learns a skill or job from another worker.

domesticate
To tame an animal so that it is not afraid of humans.

ecology
A science that studies the relationship between living things and their environment.

foster
To provide temporary care.

obedience
To carry out or follow orders.

parasite
An animal that lives in or on another animal.

scuba
A self-contained underwater breathing apparatus.

socialize
To make an animal comfortable with people and other animals.

For More Information

Books

Bedell, J. M. *So, You Want to Work with Animals? Discover Fantastic Ways to Work with Animals, from Veterinary Science to Aquatic Biology*. New York: Aladdin, 2017.

DK Publishing. *Horses: Facts at Your Fingertips*. New York: DK Publishing, 2013.

Palika, Liz. *Dog Obedience: Getting Your Pooch Off the Couch and Other Dog Training Tips*. Mankato, MN: Capstone, 2012.

Visit 12StoryLibrary.com

Scan the code or use your school's login at **12StoryLibrary.com** for recent updates about this topic and a full digital version of this book. Enjoy free access to:

- Digital ebook
- Breaking news updates
- Live content feeds
- Videos, interactive maps, and graphics
- Additional web resources

Note to educators: Visit 12StoryLibrary.com/register to sign up for free premium website access. Enjoy live content plus a full digital version of every 12-Story Library book you own for every student at your school.

Index

About the Author

Susan M. Ewing has had dogs for over 40 years. She once owned a boarding kennel and she has groomed and trained dogs. Her dogs are Pembroke Welsh corgis.

READ MORE FROM 12-STORY LIBRARY

Every 12-Story Library book is available in many formats. For more information, visit 12StoryLibrary.com.